56 Breakfast Sandwich Recipes

IRRESISTIBLE Sandwich Ideas To KICKSTART Your Morning

By Brianne Heaton

© Revelry Publishing 2014

Copyright 2014 by Revelry Publishing

All Rights reserved under International and Pan-American Copyright Conventions. By payment of required fees, you have been granted the non-exclusive, non-transferable right to access and read the text of this book. No part of this text may be reproduced, transmitted, downloaded, decompiled, reverse-engineered or stored in or introduced into any information storage and retrieval system, in any form or by any means, whether electronic or mechanical, now known, hereinafter invented, without express written permission of the publisher.

DISCLAIMER

All information in this book has been carefully researched and checked for factual accuracy. However, the authors and publishers make no warranty, express or implied, that the information contained herein is appropriate for every individual, situation or purpose, and assume no responsibility for errors or omissions. The reader assumes the risk and full responsibility for all actions, and the authors will not be held responsible for any loss or damage, whether consequential, incidental, special or otherwise that may result from the information presented in this publication.

We have relied on our own experience as well as many different sources for this book, and we have done our best to check facts and to give credit where it is due. In the event that any material is incorrect or has been used without proper permission, please contact us so that the oversight can be corrected.

ISBN-13: 978-0993969812
ISBN-10: 099396981X

Other books by Brianne Heaton:

<u>51 Dump Cake Recipes: Scrumptious Dump Cake Desserts To Satisfy Your Sweet Tooth</u>

Baking does not have to be difficult or intimidating. You can make a delicious cake in just a few steps, with just a few ingredients by using a "dump" cake recipe. Dump cakes make less mess than traditional cakes and offer unusual and decadent choices that will wow those fortunate enough to have a bite.

<u>50 Holiday Dessert Recipes: Delectable Dessert Ideas For The Christmas Holidays And Other Special Occasions</u>

Wow your family and friends with the most decadent cakes, creamiest cheesecakes, most delicious cookies, juiciest pies and most interesting international desserts! It's time to bring the baker in you to the surface and make the best desserts ever! Indulge in these holiday delights with the confidence of having made it yourself!

<u>51 Easter Dessert Ideas: Scrumptious Easter Recipes For Any Occasion</u>

This holiday cookbook collection of 51 Easter dessert recipes has something tasty and enticing for everyone, and you don't have to be Julia Child in order to pull them off. The recipes can also be used for other special occasions.

<u>46 Sriracha Flavored Recipes: Delicious Sriracha Hot Sauce Cookbook For A Spicy Palate</u>

Check out these delectable dessert, appetizer, entree, and drink recipes and see how Sriracha can enrich even the dullest of meals. Follow our meal plan for a whole week full of delicious Sriracha meals. Your taste buds will thank you for it.

Get the latest update on new releases from the author at:

htttps://www.brianneheaton.com/newsletter

Table of Contents

Introduction 1
Breakfast Sandwiches With Egg 2
   1 - Fried Egg, Bacon & Cheese Bagel 3
   2 - Spicy Sausage and Spinach Croissant 5
   3 - Mouthwatering Microwave Muffin 7
   4 - Hard-Boiled Bacon Bagel 8
   5 - Grilled Bacon, Egg and Cheese Sandwich 9
   6 - Tomato, Ham with Egg Muffin 11
   7 - Breakfast Bun 12
   8 - Hearty Crisp Muffin Sandwich 14
   9 - Bacon Avocado Egg Salad Sandwich 15
   10 - Ham and Egg Muffin Delight 16
   11 - Grilled Breakfast Supreme Cheese Sandwich 18
   12 - Simple Scramble Slider 20
   13 - Avocado Egg Sandwich 21
   14 - Sausage, Egg and Cheese Burrito 23
   15 - Spicy Mexican Pork Burrito 25
   16 - Ham and Cheese Wrap 27
   17 - Crepe and Omelet Sandwich 28
   18 - Parisian Bistro Panini 31
Breakfast Sandwiches With No Egg 33
   19 - Double Grilled Triple Meat Cheese Sandwich 34
   20 - Tomato Swiss Muffin 36
   21 - Hawaiian Get-Away Breakfast Sandwich 37
   22 - Simple BLT Sandwich 38
   23 - Swiss and Ham Waffle Sandwich 40
   24 - Apple Maple Crunch Sandwich 41
   25 - Onion and Cheese Sourdough Sandwich 42
Vegetarian Breakfast Sandwiches 43
   26 - Salmon and Egg on Pumpernickel 44
   27 - Hungry Man's Fried Egg Sandwich 46
   28 - Italian Scrambled Sandwich 48

29 - Cheesy Waffle Sandwich 50
30 - Spinach and Egg Breakfast Sandwich 51
31 - Spinach and Salsa Burrito Panini 53
32 - Cheesy Egg Roll-Up 54
33 - Spicy Avocado Breakfast Burrito 55
34 - Chili and Cheese Burrito 57
35 - Grilled Cheese Extreme 59
36 - Egg, Cheese and Tomato Sandwich 60
37 - Apple, Cinnamon and Sausage Breakfast Sandwich 62
38 - Italian Pepper and Pesto Sandwich 63
39 - Healthy Salmon Sandwich 64
40 - Cheese and Salsa Melt 65
41 - Turmeric Tofu Muffin 66
42 - Super Sweet n Spicy Sandwich 68
43 - Mushroom and Onion Tofu Sandwich 70
44 - Asian Noodle Wrap 72
45 - Eggplant and Tomato Recipe 73
46 - Veggie Broiled Sandwich 75

Sweet Breakfast Sandwiches 77
47 - Grilled Peanut Banana Sandwich 78
48 - Brie and Choco-Raspberry Panini 80
49 - Strawberry and Choco-Banana Panini 81
50 - Jamming Cinnamon Raisin Sandwich 82
51 - Nutty Brie and Apricot Croissants 83
52 - Honey I'm Bananas Bagel 85
53 - Carrot Cake Crunch Sandwich 86
54 - Grilled Honey and Goat Cheese Sandwich 87
55 - Savory Applesauce Sandwich 89
56 - Grilled Apple and Cheese Sandwich 90

Thank You 92
Other Books by Brianne Heaton 93
About the Author – Brianne Heaton 94
Connect with Brianne Heaton 95

Introduction

Breakfast is the most important meal of the day so it makes sense to treat it so. With so many choices to make, it is hard to ensure you get the right balance and variety of taste experiences.

This breakfast cookbook contains many sandwich ideas for creating something that you can enjoy every morning. Whether you're looking for something quick and easy to get you out of the door on the weekdays or something heartier with more preparation for those lazy weekend mornings, we have you covered. The varieties offered include breakfast sandwiches with eggs or without eggs, vegetarian sandwiches and sweet sandwiches.

The amounts of any ingredients in these recipes can be altered to accommodate any food allergies or personal preferences. If you're making a breakfast sandwich for yourself or for the whole family, that is not a problem. Just adjust the amount of the ingredients you require to serve the exact number of people.

Many of the sandwiches can be made with either a sandwich maker or grill. If you don't own any of those, that is ok too. With a regular toaster and skillet, any of these sandwiches can be made without sacrificing taste or aesthetics.

These breakfast sandwich recipes offer international appeal. Recipe measurements are given in both Imperial and Metric units so that people around the world can enjoy their morning breakfast.

Breakfast Sandwiches With Egg

1 - Fried Egg, Bacon & Cheese Bagel

If you prefer your eggs and bacon freshly fried, then try this recipe for a warm hearty breakfast.

Ingredients:

- 1 teaspoon butter
- 1 tablespoon mayonnaise
- 2 strips fully-cooked bacon
- 1 sesame seed bagel, split, toasted
- 1 egg
- 1 slice processed American cheese
- 1 lettuce leaf
- salt and pepper to taste

Directions:

1. If preferred, toast both the top and bottom bagel slices first.
2. Prepare the bagel bottom with mayonnaise and lettuce.
3. Place the egg on top and sprinkle pepper to taste.
4. Add the cheese slice and cooked bacon.
5. Top off with the top half of the bagel.
6. Serve warm

2 - Spicy Sausage and Spinach Croissant

Looking for a way to spice up your morning? This tasty sandwich is sure to heat up your taste buds and packs a protein punch, perfect for an after-work-out breakfast.

Fresh spinach brings this sandwich together so be sure to check the expiration dates to ensure quality and taste. If you really want to turn up the heat, add some crushed red peppers to the eggs.

Ingredients:

- ¾ cup shredded smoked Gouda cheese
- 3½ cups baby spinach
- 3 Italian sausage links (12 ounces/336 gm)
- 6 eggs, beaten
- 6 croissants, split

Directions:

1. In a large, non-stick skillet, cook the sausages over medium heat while turning the sides occasionally to ensure none of them burn for 10 to 12 minutes.
2. Once cooked, remove the sausages from the pan and let them cool slightly before cutting them horizontally to make six strips of sausage.
3. Set them aside for later.
4. Now clean the pan (or get a new one) and spray it with nonstick cooking spray. Let the pan heat up over medium heat until it is good and hot then add the spinach.
5. Let the spinach cook for about 2 or 3 minutes.
6. Next add the eggs. As they solidify, carefully pull them across the pan with an inverted turner. This should form large, soft curds. Continue this process until there is no liquid egg left, but stirring constantly is not necessary.

7. Finally, gently scoop the eggs onto the croissant bottoms and top them with a slice of sausage and cheese.
8. Cover the tops and serve them to your hungry guests.

3 - Mouthwatering Microwave Muffin

Easy and quick describe this sandwich best. No skillets and little to no work on your part are needed. When you're pressed for time or running dangerously late, this sandwich is a multi-tasker's best friend and is sure to fill you up for your big day.

To make this sandwich even tastier, sprinkle salt, pepper or your favorite seasoning on the finished egg.

Ingredients:

- 1 slice Canadian bacon or thin slice deli ham
- 1 egg, beaten
- 1 wheat English muffin, split, toasted
- Shredded Cheddar cheese

Directions:

1. In an 8 ounce (240 ml) ramekin or custard cup, spread Canadian bacon along the bottom. If you're using ham, you may have to fold the slices in half.
2. Pour the beaten egg over the bacon and microwave it in a ramekin on high for 30 seconds.
3. Carefully take out the ramekin (it will be hot) and stir.
4. Then place it back in the microwave until the egg fully sets. This should take between 15 and 30 seconds.
5. Top the eggs with cheddar cheese and serve on a hot English muffin.

4 - Hard-Boiled Bacon Bagel

For those busy mornings, this quickie sandwich is a perfect on-the-go breakfast. Though it requires a little preparation, it's worth it to hard boil the eggs and cook the bacon the night before so you can throw the sandwich together in the morning.

If you have a sudden craving for sugar, be sure to dip your sandwich in maple syrup! Even with cheese in it, maple syrup is delicious.

Ingredients:

- 2 tablespoons shredded Cheddar cheese
- 2 strips fully-cooked bacon
- 1 bagel or biscuit, split, toasted
- 1 hard-boiled egg, sliced
- Maple syrup

Directions:

1. First arrange the strips of bacon on the bagel bottom and add the slices of hard-boiled eggs.
2. If you feel so inclined, add salt and pepper.
3. Sprinkle cheese on top.
4. Microwave the bagel bottom on high for 30 seconds until the cheese has melted.
5. Place the top half back on and serve with maple syrup.

5 - Grilled Bacon, Egg and Cheese Sandwich

Finally, a grilled cheese for breakfast! This is the perfect sandwich for when you are entertaining weekend guests.

This crowd pleaser is also versatile. Try different varieties of cheeses or grill the sandwich in olive oil instead of butter.

Ingredients:

- Salt and pepper
- 3 teaspoons butter, room temperature, divided
- 1 tablespoon milk
- 2 slices Monterey Jack cheese
- 1 egg
- 2 slices whole wheat or white bread
- 2 slices fully-cooked bacon

Irresistible Sandwich Ideas To Kickstart Your Morning

Directions:

1. In a mixing bowl, whisk the egg and milk together.
2. Add pepper and salt if you prefer.
3. Set a skillet on the stove and turn on the heat to medium.
4. Melt one teaspoon of butter to prevent the egg from sticking.
5. Once the skillet is hot, add the egg to the skillet. As it solidifies, carefully pull the egg across the pan with an inverted turner. This should form large, soft curds. Continue this process until there is no liquid egg left, but stirring constantly is not necessary.
6. Remove the egg.
7. Butter both slices of bread and put the bottom slice down on the hot skillet or sandwich grill.
8. Place a slice of cheese on the bottom bread slice.
9. Carefully spoon the scrambled egg onto the cheese slice and top with the bacon.
10. Place the remaining cheese slice on top and finish off with the top bread slice, butter side up.
11. Grill the sandwich until it is golden brown.
12. Be sure to flip the sandwich only once if using a skillet.

6 - Tomato, Ham with Egg Muffin

This zesty breakfast sandwich requires little to no work on your part. Again, hard-boil enough eggs for the week on Sunday, and you have a filling breakfast that is going to make your coworkers ask, "What smells so good?"

Feel free to experiment with different types of condiments to create new sandwiches. This will keep you from getting bored with your food.

Ingredients:

- 1 thin slice deli ham (1 ounce/30 gm)
- 1 wheat English muffin, split, toasted
- 1 hard-boiled egg, sliced
- 1 tablespoon shredded mozzarella or Italian cheese blend
- Sliced tomatoes (optional)
- Dijon-mayonnaise spread (optional)

Directions:

1. After toasting the English muffin, layer the ham slice and top it with slices of the hard-boiled egg.
2. Add salt and pepper to taste.
3. Add the shredded cheese to the top.
4. Microwave on high for 30 seconds or until the cheese melts.
5. Smear the Dijon-mayonnaise on the top half of the bagel and top it off with a tomato.

7 - Breakfast Bun

Not all sandwiches are created equal, and the Breakfast Bun certainly exceeds expectations. Packed with delicious veggies and crispy bacon, this sandwich will have you full until lunch.

For different combinations, try mixing up the vegetables. Fans of spice might enjoy jalapeños and instead of green peppers use red and yellow pepper for a colorful creation. Remember, if you do not like one or more of the vegetables, leave them out. The sandwich still tastes yummy.

Ingredients:

- ¼ cup milk
- ½ cup chopped onion
- ½ cup chopped green bell pepper
- 1 cup sliced mushrooms
- 3 slices bacon
- 6 eggs
- 6 Kaiser Rolls, split
- 6 thin slices ham
- 6 thin slices tomato
- 6 thin slices Swiss or Muenster cheese

Directions:

1. In a large skillet, cook the bacon and enjoy the smell.
2. Once cooked to your liking, drain the grease into a glass jar or discard it.
3. Crumble the bacon.
4. Clean and reheat the skillet.
5. This time, add the onion, green bell peppers, and mushrooms. Let them sauté until tender, then add the bacon.

6. In a mixing bowl, whisk the eggs and milk together.
7. Once the skillet is hot, add the eggs to the skillet. As they solidify, carefully pull them across the pan with an inverted turner. This should form large, soft curds.
8. Continue this process until there is no liquid egg left, but stirring constantly is not necessary.
9. On each roll, carefully place a spoonful of the egg mixture on top.
10. Add the ham, tomato, and cheese.
11. Finally, broil all of your rolls approximately 6 inches/15 cm from the heat until the cheese is dripping off the sides of the rolls.
12. Take them out and top them.

8 - Hearty Crisp Muffin Sandwich

When you're up before the sun, it's important to have something filling in your stomach, and nothing starts a morning right like bacon. This fluffy yet crispy sandwich will jump-start your system.

If you're feeling adventurous, add a slice of tomato or a lightly grilled slice of a green bell pepper. The veggie kick will give you some much-needed vitamins.

Ingredients:

- 4 eggs, beaten
- 4 English muffins, split, toasted
- 4 slices American cheese
- 4 slices crisp-cooked bacon

Directions:

1. On a large skillet, spray nonstick cooking spray and let it heat up.
2. Once the skillet is hot, add the eggs and let them begin to set. As they do, begin pulling the eggs across the pan using an inverted turner to form large egg curds. Continue this method, but do not stir constantly. Once all of the liquid is gone, the eggs are finished.
3. Carefully portion the eggs onto the bottom halves of the English muffins and sprinkle cheese and layer bacon on top.
4. Place the muffin tops back on and enjoy!

9 - Bacon Avocado Egg Salad Sandwich

Avocados are perhaps one of the best fruits for the body. Rich in potassium and other vitamins, avocados are a good source of protein and have about half the sugar that other fruits do.

Enjoy this wonderful fruit in a sandwich that not only delights taste buds, but also won't leave you reaching for a snack an hour later.

Ingredients:

- ¼ cup mayonnaise
- ½ cup avocado, sliced
- 4 croissants, halved
- 6 slices cooked bacon
- 6 hard cooked eggs
- Salt and ground black pepper, to taste

Directions:

1. Crack the eggs into a bowl and mash them with a fork or use your mixer's paddle attachment.
2. Toss in the mayonnaise and mix well.
3. The eggs and mayonnaise should look like puffy clouds.
4. Season with salt and pepper if you like.
5. Next spread the egg salad onto the bottom half of a croissant.
6. Lay the bacon and avocado strips on top and close the sandwich with the remaining top croissant half.

10 - Ham and Egg Muffin Delight

This standard breakfast sandwich is so simple to make yet it is so tasty. In five minutes or less, you can have a satisfying breakfast to last the morning through.

Ingredients:

- 1 pinch of salt
- 1 teaspoon unsalted butter
- 1 large egg
- Thinly sliced baked ham (1 ounce/30 gm)
- 1 English muffin or baguette, split, toasted

Directions:

1. Begin by whisking the egg with a pinch of salt.
2. Melt the butter in a heated skillet then add the egg.
3. With a heat-resistant rubber spatula, pull the edge of the egg toward the center and stir gently until solid curds form.

4. Once set, fold the egg into quarters and place on the bottom half of the toasted English muffin or baguette.
5. Place thin slices of sliced ham on top of the egg and top it off with the other half of the muffin or baguette.

11 - Grilled Breakfast Supreme Cheese Sandwich

This fun grilled cheese variation combines everything you love about breakfast into one delicious sandwich. The hash browns add a satisfying layer of extra crunch.

For a more Italian take on this, add oregano, basil or Italian seasoning to the eggs. Use mozzarella instead of cheddar cheese and grill the sandwich with oil on the bread instead of butter.

Ingredients:

- 2 tablespoons butter, very soft
- 6 ounces/168 gm sharp cheddar cheese, shredded
- 1 russet potato, peeled
- 2 eggs
- 4 slices bacon (thick-sliced works the best)
- 4 slices white bread

Directions:

1. You're going to start with the hash brown first.
2. Peel the potato and set it in a pot filled with cold water.
3. Set it on high heat and let it boil.
4. As soon as it boils, bring the heat down to a simmer for about 5 minutes.
5. Then turn off the heat and set the pot aside for 15 minutes.
6. Fry up the bacon strips. Thicker slices will work best here, but it's up to you. 7. You can also make them as crispy as you like.
7. Once done, set the bacon on a plate lined with paper towel.
8. Drain the grease into a small bowl.
9. Set both aside.

10. Without cleaning the bacon pan, set it back on the stove, turn the heat on medium and crack the eggs onto the skillet.
11. You can make your eggs as runny or as hard as you like.
12. Once you finish, wrap them in tin foil to keep them warm.
13. By now, the potato should be safe to handle.
14. Grate the potato using a box shredder and place them into the bacon pan.
15. Add 2 tablespoons of bacon grease. If you're lacking bacon grease, you can use vegetable or canola oil.
16. Even out the layer of potatoes over the bottom of the pan and add salt and pepper.
17. Let the potatoes cook until they are golden brown and lightly crispy.
18. Finally, you're ready to assemble the grilled cheese.
19. Butter one side of all the slices of bread and lay two butter side down on the skillet.
20. On each top, add a quarter of the cheese, half the potatoes, one egg, two slices of bacon and another quarter of cheese.
21. Place the two remaining slices of bread butter side up on the sandwiches and grill, flipping the sandwich only once.
22. The cheese will be melted and the bread with be a light brown.
23. Serve and chow down!

12 - Simple Scramble Slider

Looking for an easy, healthy breakfast? Look no further! This microwavable sandwich adds essential vitamins and minerals to your morning diet and will give you long-lasting energy.

Don't forget about the ketchup to top off your sandwich. Combine it with mayonnaise to create a 1000 Island-like dressing for a different type of taste.

Ingredients:

- 1 tablespoon water
- 1 tablespoon chopped onion
- 2 tablespoons chopped red or green bell peppers
- 1 egg
- 1 thin slice deli ham, chopped
- 1 slider-size bun or whole wheat English muffin, split, toasted
- Ketchup (optional)

Directions:

1. Toss the onions and peppers into an 8 ounce/240 ml ramekin or custard cup and microwave for 30 seconds on high.
2. Be careful stirring the veggies because the ramekin will be hot.
3. Combine the veggies with the egg, water, and ham, and beat until the egg has completely blended.
4. Microwave the mixture for 30 more seconds on high.
5. After stirring once more, microwave until the egg is just about set.
6. Sprinkle salt and pepper on top if you like.
7. Serve the mixture in a warm bun.

13 - Avocado Egg Sandwich

This hearty sandwich squeezes in vegetables where you least expect them. The onion and avocado dress up this otherwise plain sandwich and give it a little kick.

You can also try grilling this sandwich if you'd rather not use plain toast. A Panini press might smash the sandwich a little too much, but grilling only needs about 2 tablespoons of butter.

Ingredients:

- 2 teaspoons mayonnaise
- ¼ cup of an avocado – sliced
- 1 slice sharp cheddar – 2%
- 1 slice ham
- 1 whole egg
- 2 slices whole wheat bread
- 3 thin slices onion
- Salt and cracked black pepper to taste

Directions:

1. First put the bread in the toaster and get the skillet going over medium heat.
2. Coat the skillet with non-stick cooking spray to ensure the egg doesn't stick.
3. After you crack the egg, let it cook for about 30 seconds and then carefully break the yolk. This sandwich is pretty messy as it is. The last thing you want is yolk all over your fingers.
4. After about 2 minutes, flip the egg gently and take it off the heat.
5. Add salt, pepper, and a cheese slice.
6. Set the egg on a plate and put the pan back on medium heat.
7. Lay a slice of ham down in the pan for 60 seconds.

8. Then flip it and repeat on the other side.
9. Once done, lay it on top of the egg.
10. On one slice of bread, place the avocado and onions.
11. On the other, smear mayonnaise and place the egg, cheese, and ham on top.
12. Combine them and enjoy!

14 - Sausage, Egg and Cheese Burrito

This easy burrito is also quick to make. Within a few minutes, you'll have a hearty meal with very little to clean up.

Ingredients:

- Salt and pepper for taste
- 2 tablespoons salsa sauce
- 1 sausage patty
- 1 large egg
- 1 flour tortilla (8 inch/20 cm)
- 1 slice American cheese

Directions:

1. Over a heated skillet, crumble the sausage and cook until browned.
2. Beat the egg and pour into the pan with the sausage.

3. Cook the egg mixture until the egg is done.
4. Add some salt and pepper for taste.
5. On a warm tortilla, place two half slices of cheese, end to end, in the middle.
6. Spoon the egg filling on top of the cheese and fold the tortilla over the filling.
7. Serve with salsa sauce on the side.

15 - Spicy Mexican Pork Burrito

If you liked the last recipe, then you're going to love this one. Variety is the spice of life so if you get tired of one breakfast burrito, try out another one.

Preparation is key here so make sure you have everything you need. This recipe makes a lot. Have some friends over and try the recipe on them or make these on a Sunday and wrap them up so you can easily grab one as you rush out the door.

Ingredients:

- ½ teaspoon salt
- 2 tablespoons butter
- 2 tablespoons minced garlic
- ¼ cup chopped fresh cilantro
- ½ cup red onion, diced
- ⅔ cup milk
- 1½ cups shredded Cheddar cheese
- 1 pound bulk pork sausage
- 1 can diced jalapenos (optional)
- 1 package taco seasoning
- 1 tomato, diced
- 12 eggs
- 20 (6 inch/15 cm) flour tortillas

Directions:

1. In a bowl, crack the eggs and whisk with milk and salt.
2. In a large skillet, melt the butter over a medium heat and pour in the contexts of the bowl.
3. Continue to stir the eggs until they're set.

4. Carefully chop them and set them in a large bowl off to the side.
5. Reheat the skillet and toss in the sausage and garlic.
6. As the sausage begins to cook, throw in the onion.
7. When the sausage has no pink left, it's done. Drain the grease.
8. Add the sausage to the egg mixture and combine it all with the tomato, cilantro, jalapeño, and taco seasoning.
9. Let the mixture cool for a while, then sprinkle the cheddar cheese on top and stir it in.
10. On a large cutting board or plate, lay out the tortillas and scoop the filling.
11. Place some at the bottom and center.
12. With a spoon make the mixture into a rectangle shape, flattening where at all possible.
13. Fold the bottom, left, then right edges.
14. Finish by rolling the burrito to the top edge.

16 - Ham and Cheese Wrap

For commuters, there is nothing worse than spilling your breakfast all over your new pants or shirt before a big meeting. With this breakfast wrap, however, your food stays where it should: in your hand.

A dash of salsa will liven up this wrap, and a pinch of cilantro brings a new flavor entirely. Try experimenting with other spices to see what you like best!

Ingredients:

- ¼ teaspoon pepper
- 1 tablespoon canola oil
- 2 tablespoons milk
- ¾ cup diced fully cooked ham
- 1 cup shredded cheddar cheese
- 4 flour tortillas (8 inch/20 cm), warmed
- 6 eggs

Directions:

1. Crack the eggs into a bowl.
2. Add salt and pepper then whisk vigorously.
3. Heat the oil in a large skillet and pour in the eggs over a medium heat.
4. Once the eggs have fully set, stir the ham and cheese into the mix.
5. Portion out the eggs, cheese, and ham onto 4 tortillas.
6. Roll them up and get out the door!

17 - Crepe and Omelet Sandwich

This is by far the trickiest recipe and possibly the most time consuming. The pay-off however, is well worth the time and effort put into making a stellar breakfast.

Read each ingredient list and set of directions carefully before beginning. Take your time and make sure you fully understand what the directions are telling you to do. One minor misstep might ruin the whole project so pay close attention.

Ingredients:

- 4 Crepes (see recipe below)
- 4 Omelets (see recipe below)
- 4 slices cheddar cheese
- 4 slices ham

Directions:

1. Prepare the Panini grill for use.
2. Set it to medium heat.
3. On a large, clean surface, lay one crepe flat and set an omelet on top of it.
4. The two should be the same size so feel free to trim if you need to.
5. Add a layer of ham and cheese on top of the omelet.
6. As gently as possible, roll the crepe and be extra careful not to tear it.
7. The seam side should be down.
8. Set the Panini on the grill and remove it when the cheese has completed melted and the crepe has light brown marks on it.

Recipe for Crepes

Ingredients:

- ½ teaspoon salt
- 2 tablespoons unsalted butter, melted plus more for the pan
- ¼ cup lukewarm water
- ½ cup all-purpose flour
- ½ cup milk
- 2 large eggs

Directions:

1. In a blender, add all of the above ingredients and blend into a smooth mixture.
2. Get out a large pitcher or any other type of large cup that has a pouring lid.
3. Pour the mixture in, cover the top, and let it sit for 30 minutes.
4. If you're preparing this in advance, the mixture can be stored in the refrigerator for up to 2 days.
5. On a nonstick crepe or 7½ inch/19 cm skillet, melt unsalted butter over medium heat to prevent the crepe from sticking.
6. Before spooning 2 tablespoons onto the pan, stir it up a bit.
7. Once the mix is on the pan, lift the pan off the heat and tilt it around so the batter spreads out thinly across the pan.
8. When the top appears set and the bottom looks golden, flip the crepe. You can use a spatula, but your fingers might be better.
9. After the other side has cooked, place the crepe on a wax piece of paper.
10. Cook the rest of the crepes.
11. Be sure to rebutter the pan and stir the mix after every use.
12. The crepes should be layered between the wax paper.
13. You can now use these immediately or wrap them up tightly and store in the freezer.

Recipe for Omelets

Ingredients:

- 4 large eggs
- 4 tablespoons milk
- Salt and pepper to taste

Directions:

1. The omelets should be made just before you're ready to make the final product.
2. Whisk the eggs, milk, salt, and pepper in a bowl.
3. Pour the mix into a skillet over medium heat.
4. Do not stir. Let it sit until the top looks set and the underside has turned a light shade of brown.
5. Carefully flip once and remove once the other side has cooked.

18 - Parisian Bistro Panini

Think Paris in the spring time with this fresh Panini. The apples, spinach, and brie blend well together and don't overpower the bacon.

This sandwich also serves as a lunch sandwich. Add a side of Greek yogurt with fruit mixed in and enjoy with tea or coffee.

Ingredients:

- 1/8 teaspoon salt
- 1/8 teaspoon pepper
- 1 teaspoon butter
- 2 tablespoons butter, softened
- 3 ounces/84 gm Brie cheese, thinly sliced
- ½ cup fresh baby spinach
- 4 eggs, beaten
- 4 slices sourdough bread (¾ inch/2 cm thick)
- 6 bacon strips
- 8 thin slices apple

Directions:

1. First prepare the bacon in a skillet over medium heat.
2. The longer you cook it, the crispier it will be.
3. Set the bacon on a paper towel lined plate and discard the drippings.
4. In another skillet, melt the butter and pour in the eggs and scramble.
5. When finished, spoon the eggs onto 2 slices of bread.
6. Season with salt and pepper if you like.
7. Now add a layer of cheese, apple, bacon, and spinach.
8. Top it all off with the other bread half.

9. Slightly spread softened butter on the outsides of all bread slices and grill.
10. Once the bread has browned and the cheese melts, remove the sandwich and savor it.

Breakfast Sandwiches With No Egg

19 - Double Grilled Triple Meat Cheese Sandwich

If you're a real meat lover, there's nothing better than more meat to go with your grilled cheese. This sandwich delivers on that promise. With double the cheese and triple the meat, you will be both full and satisfied.

For more variety, try different combinations of cheese.

Ingredients:

- 4 teaspoons butter
- 2 pork sausages, cooked and cut lengthwise
- 2 pieces cooked bacon
- 1 slice cooked ham
- 2 slices Cheddar cheese
- 4 slices mozzarella cheese
- 4 slices white or whole wheat bread

Directions:

1. Using a hot skillet, cook the bacon, sausage and ham.
2. Once cooked, set the meat on a paper towel and drain the grill.
3. Slice the bacon in half crosswise and the sausage in a lengthwise manner.
4. To construct the sandwich, place the cheddar cheese slice between two slices of bread.
5. Make two of these then butter the outsides of the sandwiches before placing them on a heated skillet.
6. Ensure both sides of both sandwiches are toasty brown and the cheese has melted in the center.
7. With one sandwich on the bottom, place the ham, sausage and bacon on top of it.
8. Then set the other sandwich on top to make your double sandwich.

20 - Tomato Swiss Muffin

English muffins are often tiny compared to larger bread slices and biscuits, but this breakfast sandwich dresses up that plain, old English muffin and turns it into a filling breakfast.

You can always add a few additional slices of Canadian bacon, cheese, and tomato. More protein is going to help you stave off hunger pains, and tomatoes are very good for you.

Ingredients:

- ½ tablespoon butter
- 1 whole English muffin
- 1 slice tomato
- 1½ slices Swiss cheese
- 2 slices Canadian bacon
- Coarse salt
- Ground pepper

Directions:

1. For this recipe, use either a traditional oven or a toaster oven.
2. Set it to 400°F (200°C).
3. Slice the English muffin down the middle and place both halves on the oven rack.
4. Once toasted, transfer the muffin halves to a foil-lined cookie sheet or toaster oven sheet and butter each half.
5. On the bottom half, lay the Canadian bacon down, then add the Swiss cheese and tomato.
6. Add some salt and pepper to your liking.
7. Position the muffins on the cookie or toaster sheet and put it back into the oven.
8. When the cheese has melted, it's ready.
9. Put the two halves together and enjoy.

21 - Hawaiian Get-Away Breakfast Sandwich

Recreate a tropical vacation with this pineapple breakfast sandwich. It's best to make it when you can get fresh pineapple, but canned pineapple rings will work as well.

The choice between Canadian bacon and regular bacon is up to you. For those mornings when you have less time, it's easier to warm up a slice of Canadian bacon rather than cooking several strips of bacon. On calmer mornings or weekends, however, regular bacon might be your first choice.

Ingredients:

- 1 English muffin; halved
- 2 slices of Canadian bacon (or you can just use 4 slices of bacon; two on each sandwich half)
- 2 slices of pineapple
- 2 slices of American cheese (yellow or white)

Directions:

1. Slice the English muffin in half and toast it.
2. As it toasts, set the Canadian bacon in a small frying pan and let it cook over medium heat.
3. Once both are done, it's time to build the sandwich.
4. The order should look something like this: English muffin, Canadian bacon, pineapple slice, American cheese.
5. Do the same thing on the other English muffin half.
6. You can now either toast it in a toaster oven or put it under a broiler.
7. Once the cheese has melted, the sandwich is ready to be served!

22 - Simple BLT Sandwich

This breakfast sandwich transcends breakfast, lunch, and dinner, but the bacon brings this back to breakfast. Feel free to leave off the lettuce, tomato, or mayonnaise if it's not to your liking.

This is an easy sandwich to make for a party. Once the sandwiches are made, cut them into squares and put a toothpick in them to keep them steady.

Ingredients:

- 8 tablespoons mayonnaise
- ½ lb/225 gm bacon (approximately 12 slices)
- 8 slices white bread
- 8 iceberg lettuce leaves, fresh and full
- 8 slices of ripened tomatoes

Directions:

1. Place the bacon on a skillet over medium heat.
2. Cook to your desired crispiness.
3. Once done, put the strips on a paper towel lined plate.
4. Toast the bread in the toaster.
5. As soon as it pops up, spread mayonnaise on all slices of bread then layer the lettuce with tomato on top.
6. Next place the bacon on top. You can cut the bacon in half if needed.
7. Finish with one more slice of lettuce and close the sandwich with a slice of bread mayo side down.

23 - Swiss and Ham Waffle Sandwich

Before beginning this sandwich, please be aware that you will need a rectangular electric waffle iron. A traditional Belgian one will not work, and your sandwich will not look good.

To make this sandwich taste differently, try adding jams or condiments to the bread. You can also change up the types of cheese that you're using.

Ingredients:

- ½ cup unsalted butter, softened
- 8 thin slices boiled ham (¼ lb/100 gm)
- 8 thin slices Swiss cheese (¼ lb/100 gm)
- 16 slices firm white sandwich bread
- Special equipment: a large square or rectangular electric waffle iron (not a Belgian waffle iron)

Directions:

1. Plug in the waffle iron and set it on high. It should begin to smoke.
2. Once it does, set the heat back to medium and grease it with butter.
3. Butter 1 side of all 8 slices of bread and set 4 of them butter side down on a plate.
4. Layer the 4 slices with 1 slice of cheese and ham.
5. Tuck in any ham or cheese that hangs over the side.
6. Top the ham and cheese slices with the remaining bread slices (butter side up) and put them on the grill.
7. When the bread is golden brown, take them off the grill and cut them into triangles.
8. Enjoy!

24 - Apple Maple Crunch Sandwich

Spice and sweet meet in this tangy sandwich. If you love apples in the fall, this sandwich makes a trip to the apple orchard worth the time.

If your sausage isn't already a little spicy, add some crushed red pepper to it. The two flavors complement each other very well.

Ingredients:

- 1 tablespoon butter, softened
- 2 tablespoons butter
- ¼ cup maple syrup
- 1 large Granny Smith apples - peeled, cored and sliced
- 2 slices whole wheat bread
- 3 links pork sausage

Directions:

1. Cut the sausages lengthwise before putting them in the skillet.
2. If the grease becomes too much, you can drain it.
3. Let the sausages cook for about 15 minutes.
4. Simultaneously, toss 2 tablespoons of butter into another skillet on low heat.
5. Once melted, drop in the apple slices and let them sauté until they're brown and tender.
6. After toasting the bread, butter both slices with the softened butter.
7. After draining, layer the sausages and then top them with apple slices.
8. Drizzle maple syrup on top and serve them up right!

25 - Onion and Cheese Sourdough Sandwich

The only things that can make grilled cheese better are bacon and more cheese. This sandwich delivers on that promise. With two types of cheese and some bacon and onion for a crunch, you will be both full and satisfied.

For more variety, try different combinations with cheese. You can always sub out different types of vegetables too.

Ingredients:

- 4 slices (¼ inch/ 0.6 cm thick) red onion
- 4 slices Cheddar cheese
- 4 slices mozzarella cheese
- 8 slices (½ inch/1.25 cm thick) sourdough or Vienna bread
- 8 slices bacon

Directions:

1. Turn on the grill and let it heat up for about 5 minutes.
2. Once heated, start cooking the bacon until it's lightly brown.
3. Set the bacon on a paper towel and drain the grill.
4. Slice the bacon in half crosswise.
5. Now cook the onion on the grill until it is tender.
6. To construct the sandwich, add cheddar cheese, bacon, onion, and mozzarella in that order between two slices of bread.
7. Set the sandwich on the grill until the bread is golden and the cheese looks melted.
8. Grill the other side by flipping once.
9. Finish the remaining breakfast sandwiches and enjoy!

Vegetarian Breakfast Sandwiches

26 - Salmon and Egg on Pumpernickel

For a European breakfast taste, try this smoked salmon and egg combination when you don't feel like breaking out the skillet.

Ingredients:

- Pepper to taste
- 1 tablespoon mayonnaise
- ¼ cup fresh arugula
- 1 hard-boiled egg, sliced
- 1 ounce/28 gm smoked salmon
- 2 slices of pumpernickel bread

Directions:

1. Apply mayonnaise on bottom slice of pumpernickel.
2. Arrange arugula and slices of hard-boiled egg on top of pumpernickel.
3. Sprinkle pepper to taste then add the rest of arugula and salmon.

4. Top off with the other slice of pumpernickel.

27 - Hungry Man's Fried Egg Sandwich

Classic. Delicious. Simple. When your fridge and cupboards are bare, this easy-to-assemble sandwich is both filling and quick. Grab a skillet and you're on your way.

You can change up your condiments depending on what you're feeling like. Mustard if you're tired of ketchup. Miracle Whip if you detest mayonnaise. Hot sauce if you like to wake up quickly. Get creative and turn this simple concept into a work of art.

Ingredients:

- 1 teaspoon butter
- ½ tablespoons mayonnaise
- ½ tablespoons ketchup
- 1 egg
- 1 slice processed American cheese
- 2 slices toasted white bread
- Salt and pepper to taste

Directions:

1. Over medium heat, let the butter melt on the skillet to prevent the egg from sticking.
2. Crack the egg onto the skillet and let it cook until it is to your liking.
3. Flip over if necessary.
4. While the egg is cooking, toast the bread.
5. Just before you're ready to take the egg off, set a slice of cheese onto the egg.
6. Once the cheese has melted, slide the egg onto a slice of toast and sprinkle salt and pepper on them.
7. On the remaining slice, smear as much ketchup and mayonnaise to your liking and place it over the egg.

8. Serve up your sandwich warm.

28 - Italian Scrambled Sandwich

A taste of Italy for breakfast! Pair this Italian-inspired breakfast sandwich with a cup of tea, and you'll be able to face the challenges of the day.

There isn't much of a difference between eggs made with milk or water, but a sandwich grilled in olive oil has a distinctly different flavor than a sandwich grilled in butter. Try the olive oil version for a sweeter, more authentic Italian taste.

Ingredients:

- Salt and pepper
- 6 fresh basil leaves or ¼ teaspoon dried basil leaves
- 3 teaspoons butter or olive oil, divided
- 2 tablespoons milk or water
- 2 slices mozzarella cheese
- 2 eggs
- 4 slices whole wheat or white bread
- 4 slices tomato

Directions:

1. Combine the eggs and milk into a bowl and beat until blended.
2. Add salt and pepper to taste.
3. In a skillet, heat 1 teaspoon of butter to prevent the eggs from sticking.
4. When the pan is sufficiently hot, add the eggs and let them begin to set. As they do, begin pulling the eggs across the pan using an inverted turner to form large egg curds. Continue this method, but do not stir constantly. Once all of the liquid is gone, the eggs are finished.
5. Remove the eggs and clean the pan.

6. Spread the remaining butter or oil evenly onto the bread and place two slices butter-side down on the skillet.
7. Spoon the eggs onto the bread and add the cheese, tomato, and basil.
8. Finally, cover them with the remaining slice of bread and grill them until the bread is a golden brown and the cheese is nice and gooey.
9. Be sure to flip them once as more flips may burn the bread.

29 - Cheesy Waffle Sandwich

Waffles are often a Sunday brunch favorite, but weekdays can be waffle time too. This unique sandwich gives you something to look forward to even on Mondays.

The easily assembled waffle sandwich makes frozen waffles look almost as good as homemade ones. Try different cheeses for different flavors.

Ingredients:

- 1 egg, beaten
- 1 slice co-Jack or American cheese
- 2 frozen round waffles (4 inch/10 cm)

Directions:

1. Set the oven to 400°F (200°C) and spray copious amounts of cooking spray onto a baking sheet.
2. Set 2 frozen waffles next to each other and spoon the beaten egg on each waffle, filling in as many nooks and crannies as possible.
3. Place the baking sheet in the oven and let it bake for about 10 to 12 minutes.
4. You'll know it's finished because the egg will be set and the waffles will look a little crispy.
5. Add the slice of cheese to one waffle and lay the other waffle on top of it.
6. Let the sandwich cool for a few minutes then chow down!

30 - Spinach and Egg Breakfast Sandwich

Set aside some time for this two-part recipe. It will take some time, but it is definitely worth the wait. If you're planning a Mother's Day brunch or having family over on a Sunday, this recipe is truly a crowd-pleaser.

Feel free to add some additional vegetables if you think it needs them. This recipe is also vegetarian-friendly, so you won't have to let your vegetarian family and friends go hungry.

Ingredients:

- ¼ cup to ½ cup finely minced onion
- ½ cup milk
- 3 cups grated Cheddar, Pepper Jack or Monterey Jack Cheese (or a blend)
- 4 cups fresh baby or tender spinach leaves, pre-washed or washed and dried
- 2 dozen eggs
- Freshly ground black pepper and salt to taste
- Nonstick cooking spray or softened butter for the pan

For each sandwich
- 2 slices of bread or 1 English muffin
- Hot sauce

Directions:

1. For the bake, set the oven to 350°F (180°C) and let it heat up.
2. Either spray or heavily butter a 9 x 13 x 2-inch (22.5 x 32.5 x 5-cm) pan.
3. This recipe can sometimes stick so be sure to get every corner.

4. Spread the spinach leaves over the bottom of the pan and then add a layer of onions.
5. Sprinkle half of the cheese over the onions and spinach and set it all aside.
6. In a mixing bowl, combine the milk and eggs and whisk them until you can no longer distinguish egg from milk.
7. Carefully pour the eggs into a pan as evenly as possible. You can gently rock the pan from side to side in order to get the eggs into the corners.
8. Sprinkle the remaining cheese over the top and set the pan in the oven for 22 to 25 minutes. The eggs should not have any more liquid to them, and the edges should be golden brown.
9. Take the pan out and let it cool for 10 minutes.
10. On a large cutting board, you're going to flip the pan over so the bake comes out.
11. Use a spatula to loosen the sides so the bake comes out easier.
12. Give it about 10 more minutes to cool and then slice.
13. Place a slice of the bake in between 2 slices of bread or an English muffin.
14. Drizzle with hot sauce and enjoy!

31 - Spinach and Salsa Burrito Panini

Hearty and flavorful, this Panini-burrito combo is perfect for weekend guests. The recipes are simple, and a little definitely goes a long way.

If you like a little heat in your Mexican food, feel free to add hot sauce to the burrito. You can also make your own salsa for this recipe and add the spices you like best.

Ingredients:

- ¼ cup shredded Mexican cheese blend
- $1/3$ cup black bean and corn salsa
- ½ cup baby spinach leaves
- 2 hard-boiled eggs, sliced or chopped
- 2 whole wheat or white flour tortillas (8 inch/20 cm)

Directions:

1. Prepare the Panini maker for use.
2. Lay out each tortilla and divide the eggs between the two.
3. Cover them with spinach, salsa and cheese.
4. Now make a burrito.
5. Fold the bottom edge up and roll up the tortilla firmly.
6. Set it on the Panini grill.
7. Once done, the tortillas will look lightly toasted, and the cheese will be fully melted.

32 - Cheesy Egg Roll-Up

For a Mexican-infused breakfast, try this simple microwave recipe that wakes up your taste buds with a fresh cup of coffee. Add salt and pepper if you need it.

Don't be afraid to make your own salsa for this sandwich rather than just buying the pre-made kind. Fresh salsa is chocked full of good veggies that will help you remain fuller longer.

Ingredients:

- 1 tablespoon shredded Mexican cheese blend
- 1 tablespoon salsa
- 1 flour tortilla (6 inch/15 cm)
- 1 egg

Directions:

1. In a microwave-safe bowl lined with paper towel, gently press the tortilla down and crack the egg into the center.
2. As carefully as possible break the egg, but do not break the tortilla.
3. Microwave the bowl for 30 seconds on high.
4. Take it out and stir, being extra careful not to break the tortilla.
5. Microwave once more and take out just as the egg is nearly set.
6. Lift the tortilla out of the bowl and top with cheese and salsa.
7. Roll or fold the tortilla over to create your burrito.

33 - Spicy Avocado Breakfast Burrito

Vegetarians rejoice! This sandwich is just for you. Flavorful and just a little spicy, this sandwich gets you ready for the day. It also makes a good lunch if you don't have a lot of time for breakfast.

You can always add different veggies if you don't like the ones listed. As always, try making your own salsa from scratch.

Ingredients:

- 1 tablespoon olive oil
- ¼ cup red onion, diced
- ¼ cup salsa
- 1 jalapeno pepper, deseeded and diced
- 1 clove garlic, minced
- 2 avocados, sliced
- 4 flour tortillas
- 6 eggs

Directions:

1. In a small bowl, mix the eggs.
2. To make them a little fluffier, add just 1 tablespoon of water.
3. Once they're mixed, set them to the side.
4. Next, heat a skillet over a medium heat and drizzle the olive oil over it.
5. Toss in the pepper, garlic and onion and cook them until they look tender and juicy.
6. Give the eggs one final whisk before pouring them over the veggies and scrambling them.
7. As soon as the eggs are done, spoon out the mixture onto four tortillas.
8. Decorate them with avocado slices and salsa.

9. Wrap them up and serve them hot and ready!

34 - Chili and Cheese Burrito

Get ready for another intricate, yet satisfying breakfast burrito. If you're planning on heading out for a long day and don't plan on eating until dinner, this burrito will keep you filled until then.

If you want to bring this to work in the morning, prepare all the components on Sunday and stick them in separate containers in your refrigerator. Now you can quickly spoon a little from each container onto a tortilla, microwave it, and be out the door in no time.

Ingredients:

- ¼ teaspoon chili flakes
- 2 teaspoons canola oil
- ¼ cup reduced-fat sour cream
- ¼ cup salsa
- ⅓ cup shredded pepper Jack cheese
- ½ cup small red onion, diced
- 1 cup drained, rinsed canned black beans, preferably low-sodium
- 1 red bell pepper, seeded and diced
- 1 large tomato, seeded and diced
- 1 small avocado, cubed
- 4 (10 inch/25 cm) whole-wheat tortillas (burrito-size)
- 4 eggs and 4 egg whites
- Hot sauce
- Cooking spray
- Salt and freshly ground black pepper

Directions:

1. Start by pouring the canola oil into a nonstick skillet set on medium heat.

2. Toss in the onions and peppers.
3. When the onions look soft and rubbery and the peppers appear charred, they're done.
4. Throw in the black beans and red pepper flakes and let them all simmer together for a few more minutes.
5. Add salt and pepper then spoon the mixture into a separate dish.
6. In a bowl, mix both the eggs, egg whites and cheese with a whisk.
7. Coat the skillet with non-stick spray and reset it on the stove.
8. Make sure the heat is set at medium and pour in the eggs.
9. Mix them so they scramble nicely.
10. Lay out the tortillas on a cutting board or plate.
11. Add 1 tablespoon of salsa and sour cream, followed by ¼ cup of the vegetable black bean mix.
12. Evenly distribute the eggs on the tortillas.
13. Add a dash of hot sauce and roll the tortillas up burrito style for a zesty, filling breakfast.

35 - Grilled Cheese Extreme

This sandwich is a cheese lover's dream. In order to make it as best as possible, head to the grocery store or bakery and pick up a really good, professionally-made loaf of bread. Then choose your favorite cheeses to complement the bread.

Let yourself be more creative with this particular sandwich. If you need help, ask the baker what he or she thinks would go best with their bread. You can make different combinations every time.

Ingredients:

- 1 tablespoon unsalted butter, at room temperature
- 2 to 3 ounces (56 to 84 gm) Fontana, Gruyère, or raclette cheese, sliced or grated
- 2 pieces good bread
- Sea salt (optional)

Directions:

1. First prepare your waffle iron and let it heat up.
2. Next spread butter on one side of both slices and set one slice butter side down on the waffle iron.
3. Now arrange the cheese in any way you like.
4. You can use as much or as little of each cheese as you like, but keep in mind that more is not always best.
5. Too much cheese will spill out.
6. Close the sandwich in the waffle iron, but be sure not to push it down.
7. This will smash the sandwich and spill the cheese.
8. Cook for 2 minutes and sprinkle with sea salt if you desire.

36 - Egg, Cheese and Tomato Sandwich

Try sour dough or Vienna bread for a change up. The tomato, cheese and egg flavor combination will be sure to have you making this sandwich time and time again.

Ingredients:

- 1 pinch of salt
- 3 teaspoons unsalted butter
- 1 tablespoon mayonnaise
- 1 tablespoon milk
- 1 large egg
- 4 slices tomato
- 1 slice Cheddar cheese
- 2 slices sourdough or Vienna bread

Directions:

1. Begin by whisking the egg and milk with a pinch of salt.
2. Melt a teaspoon of the butter in a heated skillet then add the egg mixture.
3. With a heat-resistant rubber spatula, pull the edge of the egg toward the center and stir gently until solid curds form.
4. Once set, fold the egg into quarters.
5. Butter both slices of bread and put one slice down on the skillet, butter side down.
6. Place the cheese, egg and tomatoes on the bread.
7. Apply mayonnaise on the unbuttered side of the top bread slice then place on top of the sandwich with the buttered side on the outside.
8. Grill the sandwich until golden brown on both sides, taking extra care when flipping over.

37 - Apple, Cinnamon and Sausage Breakfast Sandwich

Vegetarians can now enjoy this delicious sandwich for themselves. You may think that sausage should not have raspberry jam anywhere need it, but this sandwich perfectly mixes sweet flavors with hearty sausage tastes.

For an added crunch, try topping the sandwich with walnuts. The cheddar cheese might be too overwhelming for some, so try provolone for a more mellow taste.

Ingredients:

- 1 teaspoon raspberry jam
- 2 tablespoons shredded Cheddar cheese
- 1 frozen vegetarian sausage patty
- 2 slices cinnamon-raisin bread, preferably whole-wheat
- 4 thin slices apple

Directions:

1. Get the bread going in the toaster and pop the sausage in the microwave until it's cooked all the way through.
2. When it's done, crumble it up.
3. Spoon the jam onto 1 piece of toast and layer the sausage, apple slices, and cheese.
4. Add the remaining slice of toast to the top and serve.

38 - Italian Pepper and Pesto Sandwich

Feel like you're having breakfast in Venice with this delicious sandwich. Now you'll have something to look forward to before heading out the door for your morning commute.

If you have extra time one evening, try making your own pesto. You can control which flavors are more prevalent. Choose a block of fresh mozzarella over the shredded kind.

Ingredients:

- 1 teaspoon prepared pesto
- 3 tablespoons chopped roasted red pepper
- 1 whole-wheat English muffin
- 1 large egg, lightly beaten
- 1 thin slice fresh mozzarella cheese

Directions:

1. Pop the English muffin in the toaster.
2. In a microwave-safe bowl, toss in the beaten egg and roasted red pepper.
3. Cover them before microwaving for 1 minute.
4. The egg should be set, but if it isn't let it go a little longer.
5. Once the muffin is done, spread pesto on one half.
6. Add the cheese and put the egg on top of the cheese.
7. Close with the remaining half of the muffin and dig in!

39 - Healthy Salmon Sandwich

Salmon is one of today's leading super foods. Packed with omega-3 fats, salmon provides good fatty acids and has been linked to joint and cartilage health.

The capers on this sandwich are completely optional, so if it's not your thing, leave them off. Red onion is best for this recipe, but you can substitute a white onion if you prefer.

Ingredients:

- ½ teaspoon extra-virgin olive oil
- ½ teaspoon capers, rinsed and chopped (optional)
- 1 tablespoon finely chopped red onion
- 1 ounce (28 gm) smoked salmon
- 1 slice tomato
- 1 whole-wheat English muffin, split and toasted
- 2 large egg whites, beaten
- Pinch of salt

Directions:

1. In a skillet, drizzle the oil and let it heat up over a medium heat.
2. Toss in the onion and let them cook until they soften.
3. Next add the egg whites and salt.
4. If you're using capers, add them here.
5. To complete, combine the egg whites, smoked salmon and tomato in that order on the bottom half of an English muffin.

40 - Cheese and Salsa Melt

When taco night is over, you're often left with so much additional taco ingredients people didn't care to use. Now with this breakfast melt, you have a reason to use them in the morning.

If you have leftover tortillas, you can also use that instead of whole-wheat bread, but toasted bread makes this more breakfast-like.

Ingredients:

- 1 tablespoon prepared salsa
- 1 tablespoon shredded cheese, such as Mexican blend or Jack
- 2 tablespoons canned nonfat refried beans
- 1 slice whole-wheat bread, toasted

Directions:

1. Get out the refried beans and smear some onto the toast.
2. Add salsa and then cheese.
3. Pop the toast in the microwave and heat until the cheese melts.

41 - Turmeric Tofu Muffin

Tofu can be an essential staple for any vegan's diet. It has been linked to lower cholesterol and could possibly lower risk of cancer. Tofu often provides vegans with calcium and vitamin E.

So naturally, there should be a tasty way to incorporate tofu into a hearty breakfast meal that will leave you feeling full. The recipe fills that void.

Ingredients:

- ¼ teaspoon turmeric powder
- 1 slice vegan Canadian bacon
- 1 block firm tofu
- 1 vegan English muffin
- 1 slice vegan cheddar cheese
- Vegan margarine spread
- Garlic powder
- Black pepper
- Vegetable oil

Directions:

1. First cut a third of the tofu horizontally.
2. Now slice it into a square or mold it into a disk using a metal food ring or knife.
3. This will serve as the egg.
4. Heavily season it with turmeric so it looks yellow all around.
5. Also sprinkle garlic power and black pepper.
6. In a skillet, drizzle vegetable oil and add the egg and Canadian bacon.
7. When they are done, they will be brown on all sides.

8. Get the English muffin going in the toaster, and once done, spread vegan margarine on it.
9. Layer the cheese, egg and bacon on the English muffin and enjoy!

42 - Super Sweet n Spicy Sandwich

This sandwich takes very little effort on your part and will have you out the door in no time. You can use any type of bell pepper you like. We recommend green, but red, yellow, and orange will taste just as good.

The optional hot sauce will wake you up faster than a cup of coffee. If you can find vegan pepper jack cheese, your sandwich will have an extra kick to it.

This recipe calls for a Panini grill but you can alter the directions to accommodate a regular skillet and toaster.

Ingredients:

- ½ teaspoon vegan butter
- 1 teaspoon harissa or hot sauce (optional for spicy flavor)
- 1 teaspoon maple syrup or berry jam
- 1 tablespoon Daiya Vegan Cheese (optional)
- 2 tablespoons soy vegan sausage, pressed into a round patty
- 1 English Muffin
- 3 slices bell pepper, thinly sliced
- Handful fresh baby spinach
- Dash pepper
- Extra virgin olive oil (for rubbing)

Directions:

1. Make sure you have everything on the ingredients list before beginning.
2. Place the uncut English muffin under the grill press for 45 seconds.
3. Meanwhile, sort your ingredients for the upcoming work.
4. Mold 2 tablespoons of vegan sausage patty into a round patty.

5. Rub just a bit of extra virgin olive oil on the patty and set it on the heated Panini grill.
6. Take out the English muffin and close the Panini grill.
7. Watch the patty carefully as thinner patties cook faster.
8. Cut open the English muffins and set them open-faced back on the grill.
9. This will keep it warm while you prepare your veggies.
10. Take some extra virgin olive oil in your hand and rub it in the sliced peppers then set them on the grill.
11. Shut the Panini grill once more over the sausage, peppers, and bread and let them grill for a minute or two.
12. Check and take off anything that looks done, but otherwise, turn off the grill and keep the food warm inside.
13. While the sausage is still on the grill, sprinkle the cheese and set the peppers on top of it.
14. Close the Panini grill once more to let the remaining heat melt the cheese.
15. Assemble on the English muffin and enjoy!

43 - Mushroom and Onion Tofu Sandwich

This is another long and extensive recipe. Before doing anything, read through the recipe very carefully. This is a multi-step process and will take a bit of time. The payoff, however, is worth the time and effort.

As with most recipes, there is room for experimenting. You can leave off anything you don't like, but you can also vary which types of mushrooms and onions you use to give the sandwich a more diverse taste.

Ingredients:

- 30 ounces (840 gm) Prepared Tofu (recipe follows)
- Prepared Mushrooms (recipe follows)
- Prepared Onions (recipe follows)
- 3 ripe avocados, cut into quarters, sliced lengthwise
- 12 English muffins

Directions Per Order:
1. Slice the English muffins and toast them while you grill the marinated tofu to warm.
2. Set two tofu slices on top of one of the English muffin halves.
3. Place the sautéed mushrooms and caramelized onions on top and finish the pile with a fresh slice of avocado.
4. You can also add lettuce and tomato if you prefer.

Prepared Tofu - 12 servings/24 slices

Ingredients:

- 1 tablespoon sugar
- 5 ounces (150 ml) soy sauce
- 30 ounces (840 gm) tofu, firm

Directions:

1. Cut the tofu into ¼ inch or 0.6 cm thick slices.
2. Mix soy sauce and sugar together in a pan and coat the tofu in the mixture.
3. Cover the pan and let it refrigerate for 30 minutes.

Prepared Onions - 12 servings

Ingredients:

- ¼ teaspoon salt
- 2½ tablespoons olive oil
- 20 ounces (560 gm) sweet white onion, sliced $1/8$ inch or 0.3 cm thick

Directions:

1. In a skillet, mix the onions, olive oil, and salt.
2. Sauté until the onions look soft and golden brown.
3. Set aside until ready to use.

Prepared Mushrooms - 12 servings

Ingredients:

- 2½ tablespoons olive oil
- 20 ounces (560 gm) sliced white mushrooms

Directions:

1. Toss mushrooms and olive oil into a skillet and sauté them until there is no moisture in the pan.
2. Set aside until ready to use.

44 - Asian Noodle Wrap

If Chinese take-out is your guilty pleasure, you're going to love this breakfast recipe. Prepare it for breakfast or lunch if you're a late riser.

If you are having this for lunch, you can easily turn this into a salad. Cut up the chicken and toss everything into a bowl of lettuce.

Ingredients:

- ¼ cup sliced almonds
- $1/3$ cup Asian toasted sesame salad dressing
- ½ cup chow mein noodles
- 1 cup coleslaw mix
- 4 frozen vegetarian chicken patties
- 4 flour tortillas (10 inch or 25 cm), warmed

Directions:

1. Pop the chicken patties into the microwave and follow the directions on the package.
2. In a bowl, add the coleslaw mix and the dressing.
3. Set them to the side for now.
4. Slice the patties in half and set two halves off center on the tortilla.
5. Spoon 3 tablespoons coleslaw mixture, 2 tablespoons chow mein noodles and 1 tablespoon almonds onto the tortilla.
6. Fold over the filling and roll up to eat.

45 - Eggplant and Tomato Recipe

This recipe presents a wide variety of flavors and spices. Eggplant packs a good amount of protein into your diet, making this sandwich the perfect pick-me-up after a workout.

If you have the option, try using as many fresh vegetables and spices as possible. Eggplant is usually available all year around, but its season is from August to October.

Ingredients:

- $1/8$ teaspoon salt
- ¼ teaspoon dried oregano
- ¼ teaspoon pepper
- 2 teaspoons olive oil
- 2 tablespoons grated Parmesan cheese
- ¼ cup minced fresh basil
- 1 cup seasoned bread crumbs
- 1½ cups shredded part-skim mozzarella cheese
- 1 medium eggplant
- 1 garlic clove
- 2 large tomatoes
- 2 egg whites, lightly beaten
- 12 slices Italian bread (½ inch or 1.25 cm thick), toasted

Directions:

1. Preheat the oven to 375° F (190° C).
2. In a small bowl, add the oregano, oil, pepper, and salt, and then set it aside.
3. Using two bowls to keep them separate, pour in the egg whites and bread crumbs.

4. Slice the eggplant lengthwise into six pieces.
5. Now dip each piece of eggplant into the egg white bowl and then the bread crumbs.
6. Spray cooking spray onto a cookie sheet and spread the six slices onto it.
7. Bake for 20 to 25 minutes, turning once.
8. Slice each tomato into six pieces and put two slices on each eggplant slice.
9. Top with the basil mixture and finish with the cheese.
10. Put the cookie sheet back into the oven and let it cook until the cheese has melted.
11. Cut the garlic clove and rub it on one side of each toasted slice of bread.
12. Prepare the sandwiches using the breaded eggplant.
13. Serve and enjoy!

46 - Veggie Broiled Sandwich

Veggie lovers will want to make this breakfast sandwich every day. This sandwich uses Italian flavors and includes eggplant, red and jalapeño peppers, and many other yummy vegetables.

Feel free to add in your own vegetables as you see fit. White onions are always a nice punch of flavor, and tender mushrooms would mix well with the peppers.

Ingredients:

- $1/8$ teaspoon pepper
- 1 teaspoon Italian seasoning
- 5 teaspoons reduced-fat mayonnaise
- $1/3$ cup sliced zucchini (¼ inch or 0.6 cm thick)
- ½ cup sliced yellow summer squash (¼ inch or 0.6 cm thick)
- 1 cup julienned roasted sweet red peppers
- 2 teaspoons minced seeded jalapeno pepper
- 2 slices tomato
- 2 slices red onion (¼ inch or 0.6 cm thick)
- 2 fresh basil leaves
- 2 fresh spinach leaves
- 2 hard rolls, split and toasted
- 6 slices peeled eggplant (¼ inch or 0.6 cm thick)
- Cooking spray
- Dash cayenne pepper

Directions:

1. Mix the eggplant, yellow squash, zucchini, and onion in a large bowl and lightly coat the veggies with cooking spray.

Irresistible Sandwich Ideas To Kickstart Your Morning

2. Season with Italian seasoning and cayenne and toss everything together to coat the veggies.
3. If you choose to broil the vegetables, set them on a 15 x 10 x 1-inch (37.5 x 25 x 2.5-cm) baking pan after spraying the pan with cooking spray.
4. Broil in 4 to 6 inches from the heat.
5. If you'd rather grill, put the veggies on a grill and grill for 5 to 7 minutes while covering the top.
6. Turn and cook.
7. Remove with the veggies when they look tender or golden brown.
8. Smear mayonnaise on the roll bottoms and season with basil.
9. Top with spinach, red peppers, tomatoes, and jalapeños.
10. Add just a pinch of pepper before adding the broiled vegetables.
11. Cover with the top bun and enjoy!

Sweet Breakfast Sandwiches

47 - Grilled Peanut Banana Sandwich

This quick and simple sandwich provides everything you need for a pre- or post-morning workout. In small doses, peanut butter is one of the best foods for your body. It provides good fats that you need along with a ton of protein.

If you prefer chocolate spread over peanut butter, you can sub in Nutella or any other chocolate spread you prefer.

Ingredients:

- 2 teaspoons butter
- 1 tablespoon honey
- 2 tablespoons peanut butter
- 2 slices French bread
- 1 banana, sliced

Directions:

1. Heat a skillet over medium heat.
2. Butter one side of both slices of bread.
3. Spread 1 tablespoon of peanut butter onto the unbuttered side of each slice of bread.
4. Place banana slices onto the peanut buttered side of one slice, top with the other slice and press together firmly.
5. Fry the sandwich until golden brown on each side.
6. Drizzle honey on top of the sandwich and serve.

48 - Brie and Choco-Raspberry Panini

This sweet and savory breakfast Panini was meant to be enjoyed on a quiet morning. The chocolate spread and raspberries make this Panini seem more like dessert, but the brie mellows the flavors.

Enjoy this sandwich with a side of yogurt and a warm cup of tea. Fresh raspberries are far better than frozen ones, but if all you have is frozen, you can still use them.

Ingredients:

- 2 tablespoons butter, softened
- ¼ cup chocolate-hazelnut spread, such as Nutella
- ¼ cup fresh raspberries, chopped
- 4 ounces (120 ml) Brie, thinly sliced
- 8 slices sourdough bread (½ inch or 1.25 cm thick slices)

Directions:

1. Prepare the Panini grill for use.
2. Butter all slices of bread and lay four butter side down on a plate.
3. Smear on chocolate spread, add the raspberries, and top it all off with the brie.
4. Finish the sandwiches and set them on the grill.
5. Once the bread looks golden brown and cheese is oozing down the sides, take out the sandwich and enjoy it!

49 - Strawberry and Choco-Banana Panini

A fruity sandwich satisfies the sweet tooth in a healthy way. Packed with vitamins and potassium, this sandwich is a great way to get some fruit into the diet of a picky eater without him or her even realizing it.

Bananas and chocolate make an excellent combination, but be sure to try new ones with this recipe. Sub out Nutella for peanut butter and add raisins instead of strawberries.

Ingredients:

- 2 tablespoons melted butter
- ¾ cup Nutella chocolate hazelnut spread
- 1 banana, sliced
- 4-6 strawberries, hulled and sliced
- 8 slices multigrain bread

Directions:

1. Prepare the Panini grill on a medium heat.
2. Smear 1 or 2 tablespoons of Nutella on two slices of bread.
3. On one slice, add the strawberries, and on the other, add bananas.
4. Combine the two together and brush the outsides of the bread with melted butter.
5. Place the sandwich on the Panini grill and cook for about 2 or 3 minutes.
6. The bread will be toasted when it's finished.
7. For less of a mess, cut the sandwich in half and enjoy the fruit of your labor.

50 - Jamming Cinnamon Raisin Sandwich

Tired of plain grape or strawberry jam? Here is your chance to make your own delicious spread. This warm, cinnamon-infused sandwich will satisfy a morning sweet tooth.

Though apricot jam is recommended, you can try this recipe with other jams. For an extra bit of sweetness, add some honey.

Ingredients:

- ½ teaspoon ground cinnamon
- ¼ cup butter
- ¼ cup flaked coconut
- ½ cup apricot jam
- 12 slices raisin bread

Directions:

1. Get out a mixing bowl and throw in the butter and coconut.
2. Mix them together then add the jam and cinnamon.
3. On two slices of bread, spread the mixture and put them together.
4. Grease a skillet and grill the sandwich until both sides are lightly browned.

51 - Nutty Brie and Apricot Croissants

For a morning get-together or a book club meeting, this sandwich reigns supreme. The sweetness of the apricot and brown sugar is balanced with the brie, and the pecans give the sandwich a satisfying crunch.

As always, experiment with the types of jams you like. Raspberry jam goes great with provolone cheese. You can always leave off the nuts if you or a friend has a nut allergy.

Ingredients:

- 3 teaspoons dark brown sugar
- 3 tablespoons apricot preserves
- 3 tablespoons glazed pecans, chopped
- 5 ounces (140 gm) wedge of brie, rind removed, cut into ¼ inch or 0.6 cm slices
- 6 small croissants
- No-stick cooking spray
- Cinnamon sugar, if desired

Directions:

1. Cut the croissants in half lengthwise and lay a slice of brie on the bottom half.
2. Spoon out some preserves and add glazed pecans and brown sugar on top.
3. Put the top croissant back on.
4. Set a large skillet on medium heat and coat with no-stick spray.
5. Place the sandwiches on the skillet and put a lid over it.
6. Once the bread is a golden color, remove the sandwiches and apply more no-stick spray to the skillet.

7. Take the sandwiches off the skillet once done on both sides and allow them to sit covered for 3 minutes.
8. Slice the sandwiches diagonally and sprinkle cinnamon sugar on top.

52 - Honey I'm Bananas Bagel

Potassium is an essential mineral to have in your body. Without it, your heart and kidneys wouldn't function properly. So how do you get this mineral? Easy! Eat a banana!

This recipe makes it so much easier to get more potassium into your diet. You can also use a chocolate spread, but nut, almond, and peanut butter do offer more nutritional value.

Ingredients:

- 1 teaspoon honey
- 2 tablespoons natural nut butter, such as almond, cashew or peanut
- 1 whole-wheat bagel, split and toasted
- 1 small banana, sliced
- Pinch of salt

Directions:

1. In a bowl, combine the nut butter and honey.
2. Add a pinch of salt if desired.
3. Spread the mixture onto both bagel slices and arrange the bananas on top.

53 - Carrot Cake Crunch Sandwich

Breakfast meets dessert in this breakfast sandwich that satisfies an early morning sweet tooth. Though the maple syrup can be a little messy, this sandwich is well-worth some extra work in the morning.

You do not have to use pure maple syrup, reduced-fat cream cheese, or whole-grain waffles if you don't have those exact items on hand. Use whatever is available or easiest to procure.

Ingredients:

- 2 teaspoons pure maple syrup
- 1 tablespoon chopped walnuts
- 2 tablespoons reduced-fat cream cheese (Neufchâtel)
- 2 tablespoons raisins
- ½ cup shredded carrot
- 2 whole-grain frozen waffles

Directions:

1. Set the waffles down in the toaster.
2. Once they pop up, smear them with cream cheese and sprinkle the carrots, raisins, and walnuts on top.
3. Pour maple syrup on top and close with the remaining waffle.

54 - Grilled Honey and Goat Cheese Sandwich

This flavorful sandwich combines unique cheeses together with sweet honey and cinnamon bread to create a delicious breakfast experience.

You can use dried basil for this recipe, but we strongly recommend fresh basil. You also might need a little more powdered sugar so be watchful when adding the sugar.

Ingredients:

- ¼ teaspoon grated lemon rind
- 1 teaspoon powdered sugar
- 2 teaspoons thinly sliced fresh basil
- 2 teaspoons honey
- 2 tablespoons fig preserves
- 1 package (4 ounce or 112 gm) goat cheese
- 8 slices (1 ounce or 28 gm each) cinnamon-raisin bread
- Cooking spray

Directions:

1. Toss the honey, lemon rind and goat cheese into a bowl and stir until they're blended.
2. On four of the bread slices, spread 1 tablespoon of the cheese mixture and then add 1½ teaspoons of preserves and ½ teaspoon of basil.
3. Top off with the remaining bread slices to make sandwiches and cover the outsides with cooking spray.
4. Set the sandwiches in a nonstick skillet over a medium heat and flatten them down.
5. Cook until both sides are a golden shade of brown.

6. Sprinkle sugar on top if desired.

55 - Savory Applesauce Sandwich

We've worked with apple slices so far, but now it's time to use apple sauce. You can use the premade kind or you can attempt to make your own. If you have just been apple picking, make your own batch at home.

For a sweeter sandwich, add some extra cinnamon and sugar. You can use cinnamon raisin bread, but that might be a little too much cinnamon.

Ingredients:

- ¼ teaspoon ground cinnamon
- 1 tablespoon sugar
- ¼ cup butter, softened
- 1 cup applesauce
- 8 slices bread

Directions:

1. Spoon the applesauce onto all four slices of bread and combine the bread slices.
2. Spread butter on the outsides and cook on a skillet.
3. Once both sides are golden brown, take them off the grill.
4. In a small bowl, mix cinnamon and sugar together then sprinkle over the sandwich before serving.

56 - Grilled Apple and Cheese Sandwich

This fall favorite crunches like the first fallen leaves of the season. Serve with vanilla or other creamy yogurts on the side.

Confectioner's sugar can be tricky to portion correctly, so be careful when adding it. Try to gauge whether or not you'll need a little more or a little less.

Ingredients:

- ¼ teaspoon ground cinnamon
- 3 teaspoons butter, softened, divided
- 1 tablespoon honey
- 2 tablespoons confectioners' sugar
- 3 tablespoons cream cheese, softened
- ⅓ cup chopped walnuts
- 1 cup sliced peeled tart apple
- 2 slices Muenster cheese (¾ ounce or 21 gm each)
- 4 slices raisin bread

Directions:

1. Get the apples sautéed in butter until they look plump and tender.
2. In a smaller skillet, combine the honey and walnuts and cook until the walnuts are toasted.
3. Now combine the cream cheese, confectioner's sugar, and cinnamon until the mixture is well-blended.
4. Add the walnut mixture and stir once more.
5. Smear this delicious spread over 2 slices of bread and top with Muenster cheese, apple slices, and the bread.
6. Put the sandwich on a skillet coated with cooking spray and let it toast for 1 to 2 minutes.

7. Once the bread is a nice golden color and the cheese has melted, the sandwich is done.

Thank You

If you enjoyed the recipes, please consider leaving a review of the book. Good reviews encourage an author to write as well as help books to sell. Good reviews can be just a few short sentences describing what you liked about the book. If you could spend 30 seconds writing a review, I would appreciate it. You can review this title right now at your favorite retailer.

Other Books by Brianne Heaton

- 51 Dump Cake Recipes: Scrumptious Dump Cake Desserts To Satisfy Your Sweet Tooth
- 50 Holiday Dessert Recipes: Delectable Dessert Ideas For The Christmas Holidays And Other Special Occasions
- 51 Easter Dessert Ideas: Scrumptious Easter Recipes For Any Occasion
- 46 Sriracha Flavored Recipes: Delicious Sriracha Hot Sauce Cookbook For A Spicy Palate

Get the latest update on new releases from the author at:

https://www.brianneheaton.com/newsletter

About the Author – Brianne Heaton

Brianne Heaton started off collecting recipes that her family and friends enjoyed. After receiving many requests for copies of the recipes, she decided to share them by writing recipes books that everyone would appreciate.

Visit Brianne's website at:

https://www.brianneheaton.com/

Connect with Brianne Heaton

I really appreciate you reading my book! Here are my social media contact information:

Friend me on Facebook:
https://www.facebook.com/BrianneHeatonRecipeBooks/

Follow me on Twitter: https://twitter.com/brianneheaton

Check me out on Goodreads:
https://www.goodreads.com/author/show/8121938.Brianne_Heaton

Subscribe to my newsletter:
https://www.brianneheaton.com/newsletter/

Visit my website: https://www.brianneheaton.com/

www.ingramcontent.com/pod-product-compliance
Lightning Source LLC
Chambersburg PA
CBHW062102290426
44110CB00022B/2689